Woman

By Gail Marsh

Growing in Grace

Grow in grace. 2 Peter 3:18 KJV

The mission of CTA is
to glorify God by providing purposeful products
that lift up and encourage the body of Christ—
because we love him!

His Message. Your Mission.
www.CTAinc.com

Woman of God®
Growing in Grace
by Gail Marsh

Grow in grace. 2 Peter 3:18 KJV

Copyright © 2013 CTA, Inc. 1625 Larkin Williams Rd., Fenton, MO 63026-1205

Unless otherwise indicated, Scriptures are taken from the Holy Bible, New International Version®, NIV®. Copyright © 1973, 1978, 1984, 2011 by Biblica, Inc.™ Used by permission of Zondervan. All rights reserved worldwide. www.zondervan.com

Scriptures marked KJV are from the King James Version of the Bible.

Scripture marked NLT is from the Holy Bible, New Living Translation, copyright © 1996, 2004, 2007 by Tyndale House Foundation. Used by permission of Tyndale House Publishers Inc., Carol Stream, Illinois 60188. All rights reserved.

Scripture quotations marked ESV are taken from The Holy Bible, English Standard Version® (ESV®), copyright © 2001 by Crossway, a publishing ministry of Good News Publishers. Used by permission. All rights reserved.

ISBN: 978-1-935404-62-0

Printed in Thailand

Planted *with* Love

The LORD God had planted a garden . . .

Genesis 2:8

Day One

People plant gardens for a variety of reasons. Some plant because they depend on the produce a garden provides. Other people garden because they enjoy the beauty of flowers and shrubs in bloom. Some enjoy the exercise. Some find it relaxing. Reasons for gardening might fill a wheelbarrow. But always, there's a reason. And that reason often gives us insight into the gardener's character.

Why did God plant the world's first garden? Read today's Bible text again. In fact, you might want to step further into Eden's garden as you read the entire account from Genesis 2:8–25.

God, the very first gardener, plants his garden with love. See how he kneels to create flowers that will delight his people with wonderful colors and intricate designs. Watch

The LORD God had planted a garden in the east, in Eden. . . . The LORD God made all kinds of trees grow out of the ground—trees that were pleasing to the eye and good for food.
Genesis 2:8–9

s he sows seeds that will grow into plants for his
eople's nourishment.

Jow fast-forward to a different garden. This garden is
ark with sorrow, yet filled with love and purpose. It is
he Garden of Gethsemane. In this garden, a loving God
ontinues to provide for his people in his Son, Jesus. In
his garden, Jesus willingly submits to his Father's will
nd sets his eyes purposefully on the cross.

God plants both gardens with love. Peek into the
aradise that is Eden and see a beautiful first home.
ook into the garden named Gethsemane, and you'll
ee God's love personified in Jesus, his Son.

Over the next five weeks, the devotions in this booklet
vill guide you through special gardens—God's
ardens. You'll see how God plants, nurtures, prunes,
vaters, and harvests. Ask the Holy Spirit to open your
yes so you see more clearly your Gardener-Father's
eart—a heart full of love for you!

Prayer Suggestion:
Ask God to increase your awareness of
his love over the next few weeks as you meet
him daily in his Word.

Do you remember your first gardening experience? I remember. Even now, the memory is so vivid that I can almost smell the early spring lilacs in bloom. I was just a child as I followed my mother into her freshly tilled garden. Mom was planting seeds—lettuce, radishes, beans—the first planting of our early spring vegetables. My job was to follow Mom along the newly formed garden rows to pat, pat, pat a bit of soil over the seeds she gently placed into the straight, shallow line formed by the garden hoe. Pat, pat, pat. I followed along, gently and carefully covering up the seeds to protect them from harm. I took my job very seriously, and I enjoyed it immensely.

God takes joy in his gardening, too. When he first decided to "plant" you—create you—he began his task with joy. Read today's text once more. Can you picture God at

You hem me in behind and before, and you lay your hand upon me . . . You knit me together in my mother's womb.

Psalm 139:5, 13

6

work? Can you see his gentle, loving hand protecting and cradling you? Pat, pat, pat. God covered you with his hand while you grew inside your mother's womb. The Lord of life gave you life. And all the while, he delighted in you—his wonderful creation.

Read Psalm 139 in its entirety, and you'll note how important you are to your Creator, how significant and loved you've always been—from before you breathed your first breath until now, and on into forever. See, too, how your holy Father God stooped down to protect, lead, and forgive you in Jesus.

Plant this image in your heart today: God, the Gardener of all that has lived and is living. He loved you before your beginning and loves you still.

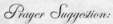

Prayer Suggestion:
Try writing your own song (psalm) of praise to your Lord. Then humbly thank him for his everlasting love. Pray that you understand and receive his love in a deeper and more meaningful way today.

*A farmer
went out to sow.*
Matthew 13:3

It felt so heavy at first—that apron filled with seeds. The sower caught up both ends of the fabric into his work-worn hands. He stood, arm muscles bunched in determination. Purposeful steps led the sower-gardener to his field. Reach, grab seeds, scatter. Reach, grab seeds, scatter. The repetitive motion took on a rhythm and became almost a song. The sun shone hot, but the sower smiled. Reach, grab seeds, scatter. Reach, grab seeds, scatter.

Today's gardeners and farmers use far more sophisticated methods of planting grain. But in Jesus' time, sowing was a hands-on experience. Read Matthew 13:1–23, and you'll discover the eternal significance of the seeds sown in Jesus' parable. Note particularly verse 23, where Jesus explains how good ground receives the seed that is God's Word: "The seed falling on good soil refers to someone who hears the word and understands it."

Did you catch it? Jesus is talking about much more than our simply hearing or having an intellectual understanding of God's Word. Basic memorization has merit, but your heavenly Father wants so much more for you! He wants a relationship. Your loving Lord wants you to know him—not just know *about* him. There's a difference. A big difference. Just look at the results in the parable!

Ask yourself: I know about God, but how well do I know *him*? How can I get to know my Savior better? What tools can I use to dig deeper into God's Word? How can the soil of my heart be better prepared to receive God's Word so that I really understand his love for me in a fuller way?

Prayer Suggestion:
Ask the Holy Spirit to become your personal
tutor as you read God's Word and grow
in your relationship with him. Then
thank him for his love.

Day Four

Root-bound? I wondered as I inspected one of my favorite houseplants. The leaves looked green and healthy. However, the stems seemed crowded within the confines of the pot, and I honestly couldn't see any signs of new growth. Sighing, I tamped the planter pot on its side to loosen the soil. Sometimes the only way to discern the truth is to get to the bottom of it all—the roots.

The plant finally tipped out, roots and all, and my suspicions were confirmed. Trapped inside the too-small pot, my plant's roots were a tangled and highly compacted mess.

It's amazing to me that a plant can look healthy on the outside and all the while be so miserably root-bound. The solution, of course, is to transplant the plant into a much bigger pot. Then, watch for amazing new growth!

Let your roots grow down into him, and let your lives be built on him.

Colossians 2:7 NLT

How about you? Are you root-bound—stuck in your too-small planter? Reread today's Bible text as you keep your own "faith roots" in mind.

It's sometimes difficult to go on growing in the Lord, isn't it? Sometimes our daily routines and staid traditions confine our growth, like a too-small flowerpot:

- The alarm is always set for 6 A.M. To set it earlier in order to have quiet time with Jesus would disrupt the routine, wouldn't it?
- It's a struggle to get everyone up and ready on Sunday morning, but to attend the Saturday night worship service might upset our family's tradition, might it not?
- A women's home Bible study meets two evenings each month. Can I spare the time?
- The prayer support group at church is looking for new members, but . . .

Feeling a little root-bound? Like a good gardener, Jesus wants to help you. After all, he loves you, forgives you, and wants you to grow, grow, grow—into a deeper relationship with him.

Prayer Suggestion:
Ask the Holy Spirit to transplant you as he broadens your vision to include new ways of growing in the Lord.

> *The kingdom of heaven is like a mustard seed . . . when it grows, it . . . becomes a tree.*
> Matthew 13:31–32

Day Five

It wasn't a mustard seed, but it grew to treelike height! I was hesitant, at first, to plant sunflower seeds. I wasn't sure that their eventual size and shape would compliment my "perfect" flower garden. But my little girls were so excited, I finally agreed.

The seeds lived up to their name: Happy Giant. Overnight, or so it seemed, the seeds sprouted and began their ascent heavenward. The girls watered and weeded and watched. We all watched, and we could hardly believe our eyes. Our Happy Giant sunflowers seemed to grow inches in minutes, feet in days. By summer's end, the plants towered over our neighbors' privacy fence.

And that's when our sunflowers first began to resemble the mustard plant in today's Scripture reading. (You might want to read the entire parable from Matthew 13:31–32.) Our neighbors noticed the sunflowers, of course. How could they *not* notice? Our sunflowers became the initial topic of conversation between neighbors who would eventually become friends. More than friends, actually. We became faith friends.

The little sunflower seeds—just like the mustard seed in Jesus' parable—proved to be a picture of the kingdom of heaven. Planted in love, the seeds grew to become a blessing to our family and our neighbors as we shared our faith, encouraged one another to grow in Jesus' love, and supported and comforted one another through life's challenges.

God's design for my flower garden was so much better than my own. He knew that seeds planted in love would produce blessings upon blessings.

Prayer Suggestion:
Is Christ leading you to do some planting today?
Pray that your seeds of faith, planted in love,
grow into towering trees in God's kingdom.

Planted *with* Love

As I meditate on this week's theme and Scripture readings, my heart overflows. This is what I want to say to my Gardener-Savior . . .

_____

_____

_____

_____

_____

_____

_____

_____

Nurtured *by* Grace

Your lips have been anointed with grace,
since God has blessed you forever.

Psalm 45:2

Day Six

Just imagine! Twenty-first century computer technology partnering with gardening, an activity as old as Eden! It's true. You can use your computer and a relatively inexpensive software package to plan your entire landscape. With a click of a button, shorter varieties of flowers are positioned virtually— in front of taller plants or climbers; shrubs requiring full sun or partial shade are virtually planted in exactly the right location in your yard—long before the frost is out of the ground. In minutes, you can see your virtual garden—in bloom!

Experienced gardeners know a computer isn't a necessity. It may take a bit longer to plan your landscape without one, but it's possible. Either way, though, careful planning is important. Good planning can turn an ordinary garden into a work of art.

A work of art—that's one way to translate the word for *handiwork* found in today's Scripture. In classical Greek, the word was sometimes used to mean *poem*. Read the text again and substitute the words *work of art* for *handiwork*.

Just as a gardener carefully chooses individual plants for a garden, God has handpicked you to be his own, dear child. He created you as his very own work of art. Awesome, isn't it? Awesome grace. When we begin to understand grace—the undeserved love of God in Christ—we bloom!

And there's more! Having created each one of us with his own loving hand, God "plants" us together with other believers. Why? So that by God's grace and in his strength, our good works, together with those of other believers, bloom to create a landscape that honors our Lord and brings him glory.

———◆————◆————

Prayer Suggestion:
Thank the Lord for the fellowship of believers he's planted in your life. Then ask Jesus how you can "bloom" in his grace today.

Grow in grace.
2 Peter 3:18 KJV

Day Seven

I'm not a patient gardener. I begin to fidget when winter temperatures warm above freezing. I mark pages in gardening catalogs months before it's time to order seeds. And it doesn't get any better once the plantings sprout. Several times each day I check to see if buds have set on, if aphids are active, or if plants need more water. I'm not a patient gardener.

So, you might wonder, why would I plant a Century Plant *(Agave americana)?* A Century Plant grows v-e-r-y s-l-o-w-l-y. Eventually this succulent will form large, pointed leaves, but Century Plants bloom only once every 30 or 40 years! Given my current age and life expectancy, it's a good possibility that I will never see my plant flower!

I'm not sure why I planted this unique species, but it serves as an object lesson for the apostle Peter's second letter—specifically, chapter 3. Peter reminds us that Jesus will return one day to judge the world. Will it be today? tomorrow? thirty or forty years from now, when my Century Plant is in full bloom? Only God, our Father, knows.

What should impatient people do as we wait for Christ's second coming? Verse 18 tells us: "Grow in the grace and knowledge of our Lord and Savior Jesus Christ." How do we grow in grace? God has already given a full measure of his grace to us through Jesus. We have all we need!

Perhaps growing in grace means appreciating God's grace in a deeper and deeper way. We can understand his grace by meditating on it, thinking thankfully about it. As we contemplate the abundance of grace God has shown to us, we gratefully share that saving grace with others. And we wait for his coming in expectant hope.

Prayer Suggestion:
To appreciate God's grace (his undeserved love to us in Christ) more fully, make an acrostic. Print the word *GRACE* vertically along the left side of a sheet of paper. Use each letter to begin a word or phrase that describes what God's grace means to you—personally! Praise him for his love!

Day Eight

For several years my family and I were privileged to live near the ocean. Not only did the beach serve as a favorite family relaxation spot, it also provided an endless supply of kelp for our garden. Kelp? Yes, kelp. With every ocean wave . . . after wave . . . after wave . . . God provided, free of charge, buckets and buckets of kelp. We used the seaweed as fertilizer and even planted seed potatoes in it for an easy, no-digging-required harvest! Kelp was organic, plentiful, and great for our garden.

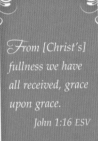

From [Christ's] fullness we have all received, grace upon grace.
John 1:16 ESV

In today's Bible reading, John mentions Christ's "grace upon grace." Can't you just see the continuous ocean waves when you picture the way God lavishes his grace on us? Time and time again, he freely sends wave upon wave of grace our way. We do nothing to earn this grace and love. God simply loves us, daily watching over us and forgiving all our many sins because of Christ's death and resurrection.

Day by day, hour by hour, God's grace keeps coming . . . and coming . . . and coming! And we receive that grace hour after hour, day after day, challenge after challenge, time after time, with thankful hearts. His grace is always more than enough to satisfy our needs.

Prayer Suggestion:
For what specific challenge do you need God's grace today? Pray about it now.

Day Nine

With plants, positioning is critical. If a shrub requires partial shade, you dare not plant it where it will receive full sunshine. If a certain variety of flower needs full sun, that's where you must plant it—not in a spot that's shady during most of the afternoon.

I learned this important gardening rule the hard way. When I first began to garden, I ignored the planting instructions that came with flowers or shrubs from my local nursery. I put new houseplants wherever I felt they made my living room look best, rather than near the window where they could get the correct amount of sunlight. You can probably guess what happened— the plants suffered and sometimes even died.

An experienced gardener appreciates and respects the power of the sun. An experienced

[Jesus said,] "Remain in me, as I also remain in you. No branch can bear fruit by itself; it must remain in the vine. Neither can you bear fruit unless you remain in me."

John 15:4

Christian appreciates the power of the Son, too. (Pardon the pun!) In our Scripture reading for today, Jesus reminds us to abide in him, to remain close to him in his Word, so that he can best nurture our souls. When we abide in him, we set roots down deep and draw up the water and nutrients that nourish our spiritual lives.

Can you remember times in your faith walk when you didn't want to follow God's directions for "Son light"? I can. I distinctly remember times when what other people thought of me or my position on the social ladder mattered more than staying in the "Son shine."

Praise Jesus that his mercy and grace never stop shining. The Bible says that his kindness leads us to repentance (Romans 2:4). When we see our misplaced priorities, our rebellion, and our willfulness, and confess these sins, that same grace welcomes us back into the "Son shine" again.

Prayer Suggestion:
Ask the Holy Spirit to reveal more to you about the security that comes from his unconditional love. Then think of a way to share his grace with someone who needs special encouragement today.

Day Ten

Some plants go in and out of style much like colors in home decor or clothing fashions. Take, for instance, hen and chicks *(Sempervivum)*. This succulent, very popular in early European times, came into vogue again during our country's "disco era." Hen and chicks, known for its hardiness and versatility, could be planted as groundcover. It could grow indoors as a houseplant. Now it has fallen out of favor again— perhaps because of its amazing ability to reproduce. And reproduce. And reproduce!

In a back corner of my gardening shed not long ago, I found the planter I used for hen and chicks when my children were young. Smiling with memories, I gently rubbed years of grime off the unique planter—a strawberry pot. Of medium size, the pot has five small pockets that protrude at equally spaced intervals all around

One generation commends your works to another.
Psalm 145:4

24

the outside of the planter. The hen, or mature plant, is usually planted in the middle of the pot. With a little care and good drainage, the hen soon sprouts little chicks—small replicas of herself. These chicks appear inside the pockets of the planter, and because of the unique design of the strawberry pot, when you water the hen, water runs down through the pockets to water the chicks, as well.

What a great illustration of God's continual grace the *Sempervivum* is! *Semper* means "always"; *vivo* means "I live." Jesus died for us and was raised from the dead, never to die again. He lives forever, and he continually gives the new life of faith to people, one generation after the next, pouring out his life-giving Word from mother to daughter, daughter to grandson, grandson to great-grandchildren, all the while nurturing faith through that same powerful Word.

Can you name three people who have shared God's grace with you? How might you thank them or honor their memory? Can you think of two or three people you yourself might encourage today with the Good News of God's grace, his undeserved love in the Crucified One? Find a way to do it!

Prayer Suggestion:
Pray Psalm 145 aloud as a prayer of praise
to your Lord.

Nurtured *by* Grace

God's grace brought you to faith in Jesus as your
Savior, but your Lord's grace doesn't stop there!
The Spirit continues to flood your life with grace
for every joy, every challenge, and every endeavor.
Think about how God's grace has affected you in
the past and how you depend on his grace for
your future. Prayerful, jot your thoughts here.

_____

_____

_____

_____

_____

_____

_____

Pruned *with* Mercy

Every branch that does bear fruit he prunes
so that it will be even more fruitful.

John 15:2

Day Eleven

[God] gave
you manna to eat
in the wilderness
. . . to humble and
test you so that in
the end it might
go well with you.

Deuteronomy 8:16

My grandmother grew beautiful
roses. They trailed up and over a
white trellis that framed the view
into her vegetable garden. In my
memory, I can still smell those
wonderful old-fashioned roses. Just
two steps out Grandma's back door,
the heady fragrance rushed up to
greet me. I sometimes sat beneath
the trellis and tried to count all the
blooms. It seemed impossible that
so many flowers could grow in one
place. It was glorious!

Given my feelings about the roses,
you can imagine my surprise one
day in early spring when I saw
Grandma heading toward the roses
with pruning clippers. I watched
from a safe distance. I'd never seen
this side of Grandma. She loved her
flowers, didn't she? I mean, this is
the woman who sang to her
houseplants to make sure they
stayed happy. What could she be
planning to do with those clippers?

You probably know—especially if you grow roses. Grandma's pruning helped the roses stay healthy, helped them continue to grow the way she wanted them to—up and over the trellis. I was very surprised to learn from Grandma that pruning was also what caused the plants to bloom so profusely! In the end, I learned that pruning was a good thing for roses.

And not just roses either. Pruning, or testing, is good for Christians, too, especially when a loving God holds the pruning tool in his gracious hand. Pruning isn't always pleasant—especially when you're the one who is going through a difficult time of testing. What matters is that in the end, God has promised to accomplish something productive in us—a stronger faith, a change of heart, a deeper walk in our relationship with Jesus.

Prayer Suggestion:
If God has brought you to a difficult time of testing, thank him for loving you enough to guide you closer to him and helping you to bloom even more than before!

Day Twelve

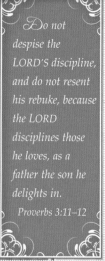

From all outward appearances, the evergreen bushes looked fine. Healthy-looking green needles formed a dense, seamless hedge in front of our home. But looks can be deceiving. Under all that lush exterior, the inside of our hedge was a tangled, dying mass of overcrowded limbs and deadwood from broken branches.

Most landscape gardeners know that evergreen hedges and other shrubs need adequate light and air both inside and out in order to grow and thrive. Without the necessary air and light, plants will wither from the inside and eventually die. Thinning the interior branches helps to ensure the plant's health and vitality.

I have to admit that there are times when I resemble those dead-on-the-inside hedges. From all outward appearances, my life looks fine. But inside I feel suffocated, even dead. All my busy external service blocks the cool, refreshing breeze of the Spirit and the life-giving light of Christ. And that's when God, the good gardener, steps in with his pruning tools.

God's pruning can be painful as he allows sickness, financial calamity, relationship challenges, and other hardships to cut away at life's deadwood. It's so important to remember that God allows these things because he loves us. He intends that hardships drive us to his Word, where he can comfort, refresh, and strengthen us, helping us to see more clearly his priorities for our lives.

Read today's Scripture verses once more, out loud. Do you see it? hear it? really believe it? God loves you. He delights in you. Most of all, he knows you—like a father knows his son. He knows what's best for you. And sometimes what's best is pruning.

Prayer Suggestion:

How has God "pruned" you in the past? How did that experience hack away at spiritual deadwood? How did the Holy Spirit refresh your soul in and after the experience? Do you know someone who faces difficult challenges today? Pray that the Holy Spirit's cool breeze will refresh and encourage that person to grow stronger in faith and closer to Jesus, our Savior.

Day Thirteen

Fungus. Gophers. Persistent weeds. These are just a few of the pests that drive me to my gardening books or to horticultural websites. I admit, when my gardening goes smoothly, I seek the experts' advice much less often. When my efforts fail—then I look for help. I'd no doubt be a much better gardener if I studied my horticultural books more often.

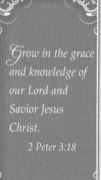

Grow in the grace and knowledge of our Lord and Savior Jesus Christ.
2 Peter 3:18

It sometimes reminds me of my spiritual life. When my life pleasantly passes from one sunny day to the next, I seek my Lord less . . . read my Bible less frequently . . . attend Bible study with less enthusiasm . . . and my prayer life diminishes. But if disaster strikes—sickness, loss of job, or other calamity—I'm driven to my Lord, often by a sense of desperation. I know this isn't the way my Savior wants our relationship to function.

It's important to understand that God doesn't zap people with diseases or disaster. It's against his loving nature. He loves us. Always. He's on our side. Forever. The reality, though, is that we live in a world sick with sin and consequences human sin has introduced into God's good creation. That means we will inevitably face hardships in this life. It does not mean God causes them. He allows them, and he intends to help us in them and bring us through them.

Our gracious Lord is powerful enough to deflect every trouble that heads our direction. Why doesn't he? Because he knows that challenges will lead us and sometimes even drive us to his Word—where he can show us our wrongdoing, assure us of his forgiveness, and empower us to change. God's Word also nourishes our relationship with him so that we can truly grow in grace and in a deep understanding of his love.

God also "prunes" us in good times. His abundant blessings fill our hearts with incredible joy, and we seek him with thanksgiving and wonder at his love. The Spirit works through every circumstance—good or bad—to draw us ever closer to his heart of love.

Prayer Suggestion:
How might your life change if you truly believed that God is on your side no matter what your outward circumstances? Ask Jesus to plant that knowledge in your heart today and help you grow in his grace forever.

Day Fourteen

I'd forgotten. I was accustomed to living in Florida, where lawns stay green year-round. So when our grass began to fade from its brilliant emerald to dull yellow-green and then to brown, I panicked. I panicked until I remembered that in the Midwest, grass goes dormant in the winter as well as in the heat of summer. Dormancy—that listless, inactive, nongrowing season when extreme cold or brutal heat rob the beauty of a lush, green landscape.

Have you ever been tempted toward dormancy in your spiritual life? I have. The temptation comes when the heat is on and troubles that have been smoldering suddenly burst into angry flames all around me. Or when worry's icy fingers squeeze my confidence so tightly that it shatters into pieces. These are times when I, too, am tempted to dry up, to go dormant. God seems so very far away.

What does dormancy look like for a Christian woman? She stops going to church or goes only out of habit and shields her soul so nothing of consequence can touch her there. She avoids faith-filled friends. She cancels her personal devotion time with Jesus. She slips quietly into the silent, spiritual desert, the icy polar cap, where nothing grows.

Our Savior, Jesus, promises in Matthew 10:22, "The one who stands firm to the end will be saved." What's more, Jesus makes enduring possible through the enabling strength of his Word. Christ enables us to focus on him—not on our circumstances. Jesus helps us focus on his power, instead of on our feelings. And while the world snickers at our faith, the Spirit assures us that the Lord is faithful. He will bring us through the toughest trials; he loves us with an everlasting love.

Prayer Suggestion:

When you are tempted to go dormant, ask the Spirit to remind you of the truth: God is faithful. He loved you to death in the cross of his Son, and he will not abandon you. Do you know someone who needs this kind of encouragement today? Ask your Lord to help you give it.

Day Fifteen

You were
sealed for the day
of redemption.
Ephesians 4:30

My backyard garden shed houses many unusual items—homemade contraptions and remedies—that are perhaps unconventional, yet essential to my success in gardening. The nail polish is a good example. Nail polish? Yes, clear nail polish sits on a small shelf right above my gardening gloves and pruning snips. And no, the polish isn't for my fingernails. I use it when I prune; it completely seals the plant where I've pruned it. Applying the polish to the wounded stem effectively keeps out insect pests and disease spores. The seal protects the damaged stem and ensures the plant's recovery.

Today's Scripture verse offers a snapshot of a similar remedy, a photo taken in the garden of God's grace. As we come through times of pruning—work challenges, health concerns, monetary worries, grief— we can be sure of one thing: God is with us. He seals our hearts and protects us from Satan's taunts. He guards our wounded spirits, comforting us by his Holy Spirit through his word of promise. He stands as our shield and defender against anything that might keep our hurts from healing.

Jesus never leaves us hanging—exposed and vulnerable—to the dangers of despair. Instead, when God has confronted us in his Word or through circumstances, he draws us to repentance. He welcomes us home, welcomes us with open, gracious arms. Our wounds are bound up by his forgiveness, grace, and love.

Prayer Suggestion:
What sins have broken your heart? Don't let the hurt continue. Don't hold onto the guilt in a misguided attempt to make amends with your Savior or earn God's forgiveness. Instead, let God bind up your broken heart and seal you forever in his grace.

Pruned *with* Mercy

As I meditate on this week's theme and Scriptures,
I want to tell my Savior, Jesus . . .

_____

_____

_____

_____

_____

_____

_____

_____

_____

Watered *by the* Spirit

*The LORD will guide you always; he will
satisfy your needs in a sun-scorched land . . . .
You will be like a well-watered garden.*

Isaiah 58:11

Day Sixteen

You will be like a well-watered garden.
Isaiah 58:11

"Dry" didn't begin to describe the drought that plagued our part of the country for four—going on five—years. Car washing and lawn irrigation had long been banned in an attempt to keep drinking water supplies at an adequate level. Brush fires posed a constant threat. Weary weather forecasters sounded hopeless and apologetic as night after night they warned of continuing hot, dry conditions. Everyone hoped and prayed for rain.

Spiritual droughts can be even more devastating, those times when gaping cracks appear in the garden of your soul, those seasons when the scorching heat of disappointment makes your mouth go dry and your spirit shrivel.

Perhaps you've survived a spiritual drought. Maybe you're in the middle of one now. In either case, this week's Scripture verse renews our hope. Just picture it! The Holy Spirit tends your soul like a good gardener—pouring out comfort, joy, and a veritable flood of promises that no matter what the situation, God's love and care for you will never fail.

Prayer Suggestion:
Name and confess the fears and frustrations that keep your soul in "drought condition." Then take a moment to picture the Holy Spirit pouring the water of hope into your soul. Thank and praise God for his power and love as you meditate on Isaiah 44:1–8.

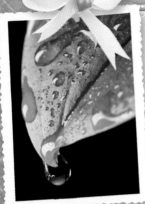

Day Seventeen

It's a gardener's dream—a slow, steady, soaking rain. The kind of rain that sinks in, rather than runs off. Rain that gently, but thoroughly, washes the dust and grime from every leaf, every petal, and makes each plant's colors more vibrant and beautiful than before. Rain that hits the earth with purpose, steadily streaming down—deep down—to the roots of every garden plant. Life-giving, life-sustaining rain.

A steady, soaking rain—that's the picture my mind paints as I consider today's Bible verse. I invite you to step into the picture, too.

Can you see yourself hesitantly removing your shoes, your bare toes stepping out onto the grassy garden path? Can you imagine catching the clear, cool water drops with your tongue and laughing as streams of mercy wash across your nose and cheeks? Go ahead! Twirl;

He saved us through the washing of rebirth and renewal by the Holy Spirit, whom he poured out on us generously through Jesus Christ our Savior.

Titus 3:5–6

42

then dance in the rain—rejoicing in God's forgiveness and grace. Kick up water drops with joy, knowing that you are clean—righteous because of your Savior Jesus. Jump and splash in water puddles with wild abandon. You're free from guilt, awash in mercy!

God, your good Gardener, sees you. And as he watches your joyful dance, he smiles.

Prayer Suggestion:
Write a personal prayer of praise to your Lord today. Thank him for his gift of forgiveness and salvation through Jesus.

Day Eighteen

I love the taste of fresh, homegrown tomatoes. This hearty plant does best when its roots grow deep into the soil, so it can tap subsoil moisture during the dry, hot days of summer. I've found that if I water my tomato plants in a normal fashion, the roots tend to grow near the top of the ground, rather than at a greater, healthier depth.

To solve my "shallow root" problem, I use a rather unconventional method to water my tomatoes. Here's what I do: First, I thoroughly clean an empty, 2-liter plastic bottle or milk jug. I poke several holes in the sides and bottom of the bottle and bury it (up to the neck of the bottle) beside my tomato plant. Every day, when I water the garden, I fill the buried container with water. Droplets seep through the holes all day long, keeping the roots hydrated. The steady watering produces a much heartier tomato plant.

God's love has been poured out into our hearts through the Holy Spirit.
Romans 5:5

Constant, steady watering . . . hmm, maybe there's a lesson that all of us can learn. Could there be a way for the Holy Spirit to refresh us constantly throughout our day? Consider:

- Reading your Bible during breakfast;
- Hearing Christian stations programmed into your car's radio;
- Glancing at an inspirational calendar or notes on your desk at work;
- Perusing a pocket-sized Bible you've tucked into your purse;
- Placing "sticky dots" on your computer and elsewhere as a reminder to invite the Holy Spirit's help and peace;
- Listening to Christian music CDs as you commute or exercise;
- As you fall asleep, meditating on a Bible promise or talking to Jesus based on a prayer book you keep on your nightstand.

Prayer Suggestion:
What can you do to keep a continual, steady stream of God's Word working in your life through the Holy Spirit? Ask your Lord's help in adapting new "watering methods" in your life today.

Day Nineteen

—✦——❧⟨⟩❧——✦—

"The quiet bubbling of a garden fountain adds peaceful tranquility to any garden setting."

That's what the newspaper advertisement proclaimed, but I needed no convincing. I'd dreamed about a garden fountain for a long time, and now seemed like the perfect opportunity to act.

I toured several garden shops and home-improvement stores in search of just the right fountain for my yard. The longer I looked, the more confused I became.

Fountains, I discovered, come in all sizes and shapes. There are stark, sleek, modern designs, as well as elaborately detailed fountains. Animals and human forms adorn some, while other fountains boast carvings of flowers and birds.

Each fountain produces its own unique sound, as well—from gentle gurgling to fierce splashing—and every sound in between. Then there are pump sizes, water requirements, installation, and maintenance considerations.

The complexity of choosing a fountain surprised me. I'm glad the fountain in today's Scripture verse is a lot simpler! Can you see the picture the psalmist paints? God's love and kindness bubbles into and over our lives through the power of the Holy Spirit. His mercy and grace splash down on us, even though we've done nothing to deserve it.

The fountain of eternal life never runs dry; it pours out in continual streams, over and over and over again. Day after day, minute by minute, the fountain pours down blessings—a deeper relationship with Jesus, our Savior, and continual growth in him, demonstrated as we serve others in self-forgetful love.

God's beautiful and enduring fountain—a perfect picture of his love.

Prayer Suggestion:
Think about the first time the fountain of God's grace splashed mercy down on you. How is the Spirit currently refreshing you? Praise and thank him for his eternal fountain of love.

Day Twenty

The gift of the
Holy Spirit had
been poured out.
Acts 10:45

What kind of gift can you give your favorite gardener? Most gardeners enjoy receiving packets of seeds, bulbs, and plant containers. Tools are useful, as are gardening books. But for something a little out of the ordinary, consider giving homemade, organic plant food, better known in gardening circles as "willow water."

For centuries, herbalists and gardeners have used this simple, homemade solution for propagating seedlings and stimulating growth in existing plants.

It's easy to make willow water, or willow tea, as it's sometimes called. Simply cut tender, new-growth stems and leaves from a willow tree. Trim your gathered foliage to 1-inch pieces, and place roughly three cups of the willow trimmings into a five-gallon bucket of water. Let the mixture steep for several days; then strain the tea-colored willow water into jars and refrigerate. This unusual gift is sure to please your favorite gardening friend.

Not many gifts are "poured out" before they become useful. But take another look at today's Bible verse. In fact, you may find it helpful to read Acts 10 in its entirety. This section of Scripture recounts the apostle Peter's visit with Cornelius. As Peter preaches, the Holy Spirit is suddenly poured out on everyone listening— Jews and Gentiles alike.

Peter made himself available to the Spirit's leading. The Spirit, in turn, worked through the apostle's message to instill faith in the hearts of the listeners. Many were filled with the Spirit and were baptized.

What do you think happened next? The Spirit continued his work—pouring out God's grace and mercy—through the words and actions of those new believers. Because of it, more people came to faith. And on and on . . .

Prayer Suggestion:
How can you better yield to the Spirit's guiding in your own life? What obstacles sometimes prevent you from passing on the Good News of salvation to others? Talk to your Lord about it.

Watered *by the* Spirit

In grace, your Lord has poured out his Spirit on you—to give you faith and grow your relationship with him. Look back over the Scripture readings from the past week. What specific images have touched your heart in a unique or powerful way? Note these images below.

_____

_____

_____

_____

_____

_____

_____

Harvested *with* Joy

Live a life worthy of the Lord and please him in every way: bearing fruit in every good work, growing in the knowledge of God, being strengthened with all power according to his glorious might.

Colossians 1:10–11

Day Twenty-One

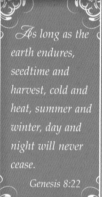

Ever wonder why gardeners garden? It's a valid question—one I've often asked myself. Especially as I hunker down in the damp spring soil, culling weeds that have nested between emerging seedlings.

Why garden? I wonder, as I pinch potato beetles and slap at mosquitoes that buzz around my head.

Why garden? is the question I hear in my mind as I wrestle my tomato plants into their cages or apply calamine lotion to my poison ivy spots.

Why garden? I ask, especially when the temperature in my kitchen tops 90 degrees because of the quarts of green beans sizzling inside the pressure canner, and I frantically search cookbooks for new and exciting ways to use up the never-ending supply of zucchini.

Most gardeners garden because of the harvest—fresh fruit, ripe from the tree; snappy vegetables, bursting with flavor; or beautiful bouquets of fragrant, homegrown flowers. It's the harvest. It's all about the harvest.

The harvest is a reminder of the cycle we call life. Read Genesis 8:22 once more. There is a sure and abiding comfort in this verse. It's a promise that helps keep me focused on the real reason for living—God is growing me for his harvest. There will be difficulties—summer, slugs, and sadness; winter, weeds, and worries—but as long as the earth remains and I have life, God will be with me.

When I'm in the cold, my Savior will provide the warmth of his forgiveness and love. Nighttime need not frighten me, because I know that as I sleep, my God will not. And in the end—the very end—God will gather up his harvest. It will be a great and joy-filled harvest of believers in Jesus, the Savior.

Prayer Suggestion:
Picture yourself in the final harvest of believers.
Ask Jesus to help you live today with that final
harvest in mind.

Day Twenty-Two

Timing is everything. If you want to enjoy your garden year-round, plant the right types of flowers, trees, and bushes, and you can enjoy color in your yard from January to December and every month in between. Planting the right combination of vegetables at the right time can ensure garden-fresh eating for months!

The Bible verse for today reminds us that every living thing brings forth its unique fruit in its season—at the proper time. I wonder if the same holds true for the harvest of "fruit" in our own lives. Here's what I mean: When I was young, I wished I were older so that I could sing in our church choir. About the time I was old enough to join the choir, I wished I were a teacher in a Christian school. When I was old enough to become a Christian teacher, I dreamed about serving as a missionary. And on it went. As I

> *That person is like a tree planted by streams of water, which yields its fruit in season.*
>
> Psalm 1:3

continually looked to the future, I failed to act on current opportunities for service—the "here-and-now harvest."

Don't misunderstand—I think dreams and aspirations are fine. I also know that preparation and maturity are sometimes a prerequisite for certain types of service. But merely waiting for the right time might mean missing an opportunity in the here and now, an opportunity that's lost forever. It's great to work toward a goal, but the Holy Spirit also wants us to be open to fruit-bearing opportunities all along the way.

Prayer Suggestion:
Are you waiting for a more opportune "harvest time" in your own life? Could God be opening a door for service for you today? Ask him to help you see possibilities for fruit-bearing in your life right now.

Day Twenty-Three

You need more than seeds to grow trees—you also need patience and longevity. That's because trees are very slow growers. If I plant a small sapling today, even if weather conditions are perfect, disease and pests are absent, and the sapling itself is from healthy stock, I still may not live long enough to see that tree reach maturity.

Why, then, do I plant trees? Because I love them! I know how good it feels to sit under a tree's shade. I love hearing the breeze whisper through the branches. I appreciate the strength and solid rootedness a tree represents. Will I see my trees reach maturity? I don't know, but I intend to keep planting them!

The sower in today's Bible reading isn't planting trees, but he demonstrates the patience and faith of a person who plants seeds of a different type—seeds of faith that

Those who sow with tears will reap with songs of joy. Those who go out weeping, carrying seed to sow, will return with songs of joy, carrying sheaves with them.

Psalm 126:5–6

are sown as the Word of God is shared with others. Even though the job sometimes brings the sower to tears, he nevertheless keeps on planting.

Where are you sowing the seeds of God's Word? At work? With family members or friends? Do you ever feel discouraged? Then why sow seeds? Why share God's Word? Because you know what it's like to be held securely in your Savior's arms and you love how the Holy Spirit whispers encouragement into your life. You've come to appreciate and depend upon your heavenly Father's strength and love. And you want others to experience all these good gifts of God, too!

Most of all, we keep sowing the seeds of the Word because God has promised a harvest:

[The LORD says,] my word . . . will not return to me empty, but will accomplish what I desire and achieve the purpose for which I sent it. Isaiah 55:11

Prayer Suggestion:
Pray today for people who need to hear and believe the Good News of salvation through Jesus. Pray for steadfastness in sowing, too.

There's a sense of excitement and anticipation as harvest time nears. Days, even weeks before I plan to harvest from my garden, I begin to prepare. I collect my harvesting "tools"—like laundry baskets. Yes, I said laundry baskets.

I like to use my large plastic laundry baskets when I pick fruits and veggies. When I've gathered the apples or carrots in the basket, I can easily wash them. I just spray water from the garden hose over the basket of harvested vegetables. It saves time and keeps most of the mess outside the house.

As harvest approaches, I also take stock of my pantry. I count and check canning jars, shop for freezer bags and canning lids, and clear my freezer and basement shelves to make way for the new harvest.

Getting ready for harvest time is necessary and exciting! Preparing

Let the fields be jubilant, and everything in them; let all the trees of the forest sing for joy. Let all creation rejoice before the LORD, for he comes.

Psalm 96:12–13

heightens my sense of purpose and joy in gardening.

Psalm 96 reminds me of a different kind of harvest—the return of our Lord and Savior, Jesus, on Judgment Day. On that day, the psalmist tells us, the heavens will rejoice and the earth will be glad. The fields will be jubilant and the trees of the forest will sing for joy! You might want to read the entire psalm to catch the excitement.)

One day the final harvest will come. What a privilege that God invites us to have a part in preparing for it. Remembering that, all believers share a Spirit-given sense of purpose. We want everyone in the world to know the Savior! We seek the Spirit's strength so that we remain faithful to Christ no matter what happens. And we ask the Holy Spirit to give us a sense of joyful anticipation, knowing that eternal life in heaven awaits us and all believers in Jesus, our risen and reigning Lord.

Prayer Suggestion:
Ask your Lord Jesus to help you live purposefully today in preparation for his final harvest.

Plink! Plink! Plink! It's the sound every gardener loves to hear. Plink! It's like music to my ears, and it brings a smile to my lips every time I hear it. All the hard work and months of planting, weeding, harvesting are rewarded with that one little sound. Plink!

"Plink" is the sound a canning lid makes when the fruit or vegetables have been pressure cooked or canned for preservation. The "plink" tells me that the jar is sealed, and the food inside the jar will keep for months or even years without spoiling.

Read today's Bible verse again. Can you hear a "plink"? It's the reassuring sound of God's faithful promise—his promise to preserve us until Christ returns. Note the word *blameless*—not one tiny imperfection or blemish can be found on believers preserved in

May God himself, the God of peace, sanctify you through and through. May your whole spirit, soul and body be kept blameless at the coming of our Lord Jesus Christ.
1 Thes. 5:23

esus. That's because he took all our sins to his cross
and buried them in his grave forever. Christ's
resurrection preserves us even through physical death.
esus keeps us safe until our own resurrection to eternal
oy with him and all believers.

Completely forgiven by God's grace, preserved by his
ove and power, we eagerly look forward to our eternal
home with Jesus and one another in heaven. Plink!

Prayer Suggestion:
Kneel or sit before your Lord and King, Jesus. Praise
him for preserving the believers who have shared his
message of grace with you in the past. Ask the Holy
Spirit to inspire you to share this same saving
message with others and preserve you in the true
faith until you greet your Master Gardener
face-to-face.

Harvested *with* Joy

Reflect on the themes: planted with love; nurtured by grace; pruned with mercy; watered by the Spirit, and harvested with joy. Then think about the truths the Holy Spirit has impressed upon your heart as you've studied each theme. Record your thoughts on the lines below, and pray about how you might share these truths with others.

_____

_____

_____

_____

_____

_____

_____

_____

For You—
Grace!

Grace and peace to you from God our
Father and from the Lord Jesus Christ.
Romans 1:7

In him we have redemption through his blood, the
forgiveness of sins, in accordance with the riches of
God's grace. Ephesians 1:7

My grace is sufficient for you. 2 Corinthians 12:9

Let us then approach God's throne of grace with
confidence, so that we may receive mercy
and find grace. Hebrews 4:16

Now I commit you to God and to the word of his
grace, which can build you up and give you an
inheritance among all those who are sanctified.
Acts 20:32

This grace was given us in Christ Jesus before the
beginning of time, but it has now been revealed
through the appearing of our Savior, Christ Jesus.
2 Timothy 1:9–10

You know the grace of our Lord Jesus Christ, that
though he was rich, yet for your sake he became poor,
so that you through his poverty might become rich.
2 Corinthians 8:9

To see all of CTA's books or request a catalog, visit us at www.CTAinc.com.

If this book has made a difference in your life or if you have simply enjoyed it, we would like to hear from you. Your words will encourage us! If you have suggestions for us to consider as we create books like this in the future, please send those, too.

We invite you to post your comments at http://share.ctainc.com/ or on our Facebook page at http://www.facebook.com/CTAinc

Or you can reach us by e-mail at editor@CTAinc.com. Please include the subject line: WOG3SC

You can also contact us at:

Editorial Coordinator
Department WOG3SC
CTA, Inc.
P.O. Box 1205
Fenton, MO 63026-1205